INVENT YOUR FUTURE

Take Your Life from the Ordinary
to the Extraordinary!

Russ Peak

INVENT YOUR FUTURE

TAKE YOUR LIFE FROM THE ORDINARY TO THE EXTRAORDINARY

Invent Publishing

Post Office Box 207

McMinnville, OR   97128-0207   U.S.A.

Orders@InventPublishing.com; http://www.InventPublishing.com

Copyright © 2008 by Russ Peak

Invent Your Future Keynote Available

Russ Peak Presentations

Toll Free: (800) 381-5858

www.RussPeak.com

All rights reserved. No part of this book may be reproduced or transmitted in any form or by any means, electronic or mechanical, including photocopying, recording or by any information storage and retrieval system, without written permission of the author, except for the inclusion of brief quotation in a review.

Library of Congress Cataloging-in-Publication Data

Peak, Russ.

INVENT YOUR FUTURE:

TAKE YOUR LIFE FROM THE ORDINARY TO THE EXTRAORDINARY / by Russ Peak

ISBN-13: 978-0-9816674-0-9

To Megan & Grace

You make me so proud!

I am excited to watch you grow into the wonderful young ladies you are destined to be.

ACKNOWLEDGEMENTS

To Ron Ippolitto for helping me take my disorganized pile of ideas and stories and turn it into this book. You are a good friend. I couldn't have done it without you.

To the students, teachers, and advisors with whom I have had the pleasure to work - You have given me the opportunity to come into your world and allowed me to speak to your students on your campus and at your conferences. Thank you for friendship, your support, and your trust.

To the professional speakers, entertainers, and authors who have guided me and been a positive influence in my speaking and in my life. Whether you know it or not, so many of you have helped shape my career and kept me on the right path. In particular, the "Original" Mike Smith, Scott Greenberg, Stu Shaffer, Patrick George, Dr. Earl Reum, and our recently departed friend Bob Burton.

To my wife Allie - I love you. You are my best friend, my inspiration, and the most amazing person I know. Thank you for believing in me and for your encouragement.

TABLE OF CONTENTS

1. THE ADVENTURE BEGINS 9
2. WHAT IS SUCCESS? 15
3. RESPONSIBILITY 23
4. WHO NEEDS GOALS? 33
5. WHAT DO YOU REALLY WANT? 39
6. LET'S SET SOME GOALS 49
7. BREAKING IT DOWN 61
8. JUST DO IT! 77
9. STAY ON COURSE 83
10. THE POWER OF BELIEF 89
11. CLEAN UP YOUR ACT 107
12. IGNITE YOUR IMAGINATION 113
13. KEEP MOVING FORWARD 123
14. A FEW LAST WORDS 131

1. THE ADVENTURE BEGINS

As I made my way through the winding marketplace of the remote village of Tepotzlan, Mexico, I hurried to where I had spotted a large crowd. From its center I could hear a loud voice. I wedged my way in among the excited onlookers. The undivided focus of their attention was paid to a man standing next to a pushcart. He held in his hand a cheaply made cross that hung on a thin chain. A few dozen identical crosses hung on pegs on the cart.

It was not the cross itself that held the audience but the words the man spoke. "This cross has been blessed so that you may also be blessed. With this cross your crops will grow strong, your family will have health, and bad omens will turn their backs to your home." I couldn't believe my eyes, it was a modern-day snake oil salesman — a medicine show. The crowd hung onto his every word. "A man's sister, she had a terrible illness. The doctors and las curandaras (spiritualists) all said she was not to be cured. Yet she wore the cross around her neck for a day and she was healed." The man produced from his cart a large glass of dark blue water and held it up for all to see. "Watch and see the power of God's blessings, which have been placed upon this cross!" He dropped the cross into the glass of water and instantly the water turned clear. The crowd went wild, producing their hard-earned pesos, waving them in the air, eager to purchase one of his charms. The man graciously parted with these objects of God's miracles for a Mexican equivalent of twelve American dollars each.

If I hadn't seen it with my own eyes, I would have thought that what happened in that village was like a scene out of a book. It was the summer of my second year of college and I decided to head south of the border to Mexico. I was looking for excitement. I had taken enough Spanish classes to get me where I wanted to go and had studied every travel guide I could get my hands on. Moreover, I watched *Raiders of the Lost Ark* like a hundred times! The result was the first of many summers filled with climbing Aztec pyramids, exploring gorgeous beaches, and enjoying Mexican food like you'll find nowhere else than where it originated. I had a blast! That's where I discovered...

LIFE IS A DARING ADVENTURE!

World travel may not be your thing, but whether exploring other countries, or your own school campus... Life is an adventure - but only if you make it so. That's why I laugh when so many people - when

THE ADVENTURE BEGINS

they contemplate their life – say "Hmmm... I never saw anything good." That's ridiculous! There are so many incredible things to do, people to meet, sights to see, and lessons to learn. The opportunities are endless!

That's what this book is about. I want to challenge you to go through life with your eyes wide open and ready for adventure. When you do, it will come. The best thing is that it won't take years or months until you're ready to head out on your adventure. It begins now.

When I witnessed the scene of the charlatan in Mexico, I was absolutely amazed. Not at the power of the 'magical charm' he was selling – I had the same trick of changing the color of water included in my childhood magic set. Rather, I was amazed at his customers, and their eagerness to get their hands on an object that would solve all their worries in an effortless instant. However, that should come as no surprise. People are always looking for the easy way out. My middle school history teacher would tell us that we spent twenty times more effort trying to get out of our homework than if we had just done the homework itself. Likewise, in an effort to obtain a supernatural shortcut to success, the villagers simply wasted a month's salary on a worthless trinket decorated with a misleading tale. That's called irony. Unfortunately, the reality of a magical amulet that will bring all our dreams to us does not exist. Success takes effort. Even more unfortunate is that some people will keep wasting their time and effort deceived by such foolish illusions again and again.

INVENT YOUR FUTURE

So what are you going to find in this book? You will not find a magic cross that will accomplish your dreams for you. Nor will you find it full of intuitive development exercises, empty success promises, or metaphysical mumbo jumbo that could mislead you into thinking that with enough positive thought your dreams will effortlessly find you. Unfortunately, this is the type of nonsense that has become commonplace among the books filling the bookstore shelves. These books that promise instant, effortless success are usually as authentic as that charlatan's cross. The truth of the matter is that although the technique and discipline to accomplish all your goals is within your grasp, it will take a little effort. It might even take a lot of effort. There is not an instant path to success. You will have to work for it.

Luckily, within these pages are practical yet simple principles you can use to make your journey to success quicker and easier. Whether this is your first attempt trying to take control of your future or if you are simply trying to reassess your priorities, the goal of this book is to help you learn about yourself, figure out what you want out of life, and when you've done that, to define and invent your future.

Do the exercises included in this book — really do them. This book is filled with places where you will be asked to write your ideas and fill in the blanks to explore your own personal goals and stretch your creativity. If you follow these easy steps, you will be on your way to the life you have always imagined.

THE ADVENTURE BEGINS

ACTION STEP

This chapter has only one simple exercise.

Chose one of the following:

A.   You are willing to do a little hard work in order to invent a new future for yourself.

B.   You want the address of the guy that sells a magic cross.

If your answer is **A**, keep reading. Let the adventure begin.

If your answer is **B** then return this book or give it to a friend.

It's not for you.

INVENT YOUR FUTURE

2. WHAT IS SUCCESS?

One day a fisherman was lying on a beautiful beach with his fishing pole propped up in the sand and his solitary line cast out into the sparkling blue surf. He was enjoying the warmth of the afternoon sun and the prospect of catching a fish or two over the course of the afternoon.

About that time, a businessman came walking down the beach, trying to relieve some of the stress of his workday. He noticed the fisherman sitting on the beach and decided to find out why this fisherman was fishing instead of working harder to make a living for himself and his family. "You aren't going to catch many fish that way," said the businessman to the fisherman. "You should be working rather than lying on the beach!"

The fisherman looked up at the businessman, smiled, and replied, "And what will my reward be?"

"Well, you can get bigger nets and catch more fish!" was the businessman's answer.

"And then what will my reward be?" asked the fisherman, still smiling.

The businessman replied, "You will make money and you'll be able to buy a boat, which will then result in larger catches of fish!"

"And then what will my reward be?" asked the fisherman again. The businessman was beginning to get a little irritated with the fisherman's questions. "You can buy a bigger boat, and hire some people to work for you!" he said.

"And then what will my reward be?" repeated the fisherman.

The businessman was getting angry. "Don't you understand? You can build up a fleet of fishing boats, sail all over the world, and let all your employees catch fish for you!"

Once again the fisherman asked, "And then what will my reward be?"

The businessman was red with rage and shouted at the fisherman, "Don't you understand that you can become so rich you will never have to work for your living again! You can spend all the rest of your days sitting on this beach, looking at the sunset. You won't have a care in the world!"

WHAT IS SUCCESS?

The fisherman, still smiling, looked up and said, "And what do you think I'm doing right now?"

THE DEFINITION OF SUCCESS IS YOURS

Success is a strange word. We hear about success all the time. We hear tales about people who are a success. We hear about products, movies, and companies that are considered a success. Most of us want to be a success, but lots of us don't know what it means to be a success. That's probably because the definition can be defined in a number of ways. In fact, if you were to ask everyone you came across during your average day, you would find that each person you asked would give you a slightly different answer than the last. Some will explain that success comes from money, power, fame, spirituality, possessions, education, all of the above, or none of the above. People have died, countries have gone to war, and families have been divided over "success."

In our story of the businessman and the fisherman, each had conflicting ideas of the meaning of success. Who can say who is right? Some people may think their story explains it all... some might strongly disagree. To the fisherman, it came by skipping to the end of the story. Laying on the beach without a care it the world summed it up for him. Is that the case for you? Maybe you'd find that sort of life boring and prefer to find success is in the journey: the challenge of school, being part of a family, traveling to different countries, the work it takes to succeed as an athlete, or perhaps helping others or working for a cause.

Here are a few ideas of how others have defined success:

> "All I think is if you can find work, stay healthy, find somebody to share it with, you're the ultimate success."
>
> Dick Clark

> "Son, being popular is the most important thing in the world."
>
> Homer Simpson (to Bart)

> "You are a success when you can look back in forgiveness, forward in hope, down in compassion, and up with gratitude."
>
> Zig Ziglar

> "Life is a game. The one who with the most toys wins."
>
> Unknown

WHAT IS SUCCESS?

"A man is a success if he gets up in the morning and goes to bed at night and in between does what he wants to do."

Bob Dylan

"Success is being all you can be in each area of your life without sacrificing your ability to be all you can in each and every other area of life."

Larry Winget

"To laugh often and much; to win the respect of intelligent people and affection of children; to appreciate beauty; to find the best in others; to leave the world a bit better, whether by a healthy child, a garden patch or a redeemed social condition; to know even one life has breathed easier because you lived. This is to succeed!"

Ralph Waldo Emerson

"Success? I just want a sandwich named after me."

Jon Stewart

Again, you can see there are so many definitions of success no one could possibly tell you which one you must choose. I can tell you that when you get there, you will know it. You may already know what success means to you. Perhaps one of the above descriptions fits you perfectly. If so, then you're already a long way down the path of success. On the other hand, if you have no idea of what success means to you, don't worry.

In the following action steps, you'll explore your inner-self, and perhaps get closer to finding your personal definition of success.

ACTION STEP

Write down five to ten words you think are key elements to success. For example you could write: money, a degree, a best-selling novel, true love, having children, or following God. Whatever you write - be honest. Don't just write how 'the world' defines success. Explore elements that define it for you.

1. _____

2. _____

3. _____

4. _____

5. _____

6. _____

7. _____

8. _____

9. _____

10. _____

INVENT YOUR FUTURE

ACTION STEP

Now, using as many of the words as you can that you've decided are key elements, create your own definition of success. You can write it like the success quotes earlier in the chapter. You can start it off with one of the following...

> I will feel like a success when I...

> I know I am living a successful life if I am...

If those don't work for you, try one of your own.

3. RESPONSIBILITY

Anyone who wants to invent their future has to learn this important lesson:

Each of us must accept responsibility for the current position of our own life.

I learned this lesson from Mr. Champagne, my senior year civics teacher, who explained to me that if I am pulled over by a police officer for speeding, I have no right to complain to the officer that giving me a ticket isn't fair. I knew that speeding was illegal and I made the choice to speed. It wouldn't be his fault. And it wouldn't be my car's fault. So I should just take the ticket like a man. I understood my teacher's point and agreed. Yet at the time I wished he wasn't using this scenario to illustrate the reason behind his decision to give me a lower mark on an assignment, which I had chosen to turn in a day late.

INVENT YOUR FUTURE

Perhaps you are struggling with the "uncontrollable" right now. It could be the death of a close relative, dealing with a disability, your parents' divorce, an insufferable boss, or the difficulty of finding a part-time job due to a suffering economy. Yes, those things are beyond your control. Sometimes you will be given situations that seem just plain unfair. However, taking control of your future means accepting that although tough times happen, you are still the one accountable for how you react to and deal with these situations. When things get tough, nobody can make you either lie down in defeat or fight back with all your might. That choice is completely up to you.

Taking responsibility for your current situation is not an easy task, but it is a crucial step in becoming the inventor of your future. It is hard to look at yourself and discover that the reason why your life is not exactly where you want it to be might be the result of your own choices.

Like it or not... Here are three facts that are key to inventing your future:

1) **YOU ARE RESPONSIBLE FOR YOUR CHOICES.**
   (no matter what others may do.)

2) **YOU ARE RESPONSIBLE FOR YOUR OWN ATTITUDE.**

3) **YOU ARE RESPONSIBLE FOR WHO YOU ARE.**

In other words, if you're not satisfied, it may be your own fault. Have you taken the necessary steps toward a desirable change?

Quit Making Excuses

Excuses may make you feel better for a while. Yet, excuses cripple your ability to make changes, correct problems, or to invent your future. It's a loser's game. Don't make excuses. Accept responsibility for yourself and enable your ability to make meaningful change. Maybe you got a poor grade because your teacher was completely unreasonable and would not accept your assignment a day late. Suppose you had turned it in on time. It was a choice that you made. You had control. It was your choice. There may have been many factors but the point is that you had the power to determine the outcome.

Of course, not everything is under your control. But many things are, and those are the things you should concentrate on. Furthermore, many of those things can shape the outcome of your future. The sooner you accept responsibility for these things, the quicker you'll be on your way to inventing your future. When you fail to accept responsibility, you have given up the power. You have hurt yourself.

Even our founding fathers didn't buy excuses. I'm sure they were met by plenty of them when they worked to create the greatest country in the world.

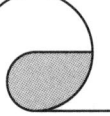

"Ninety-nine percent of the failures come from people who have the habit of making excuses."

George Washington

"He that is good for making excuses is seldom good for anything else."

Benjamin Franklin

You Can Be Right or You Can Be Happy

Mike was a sophomore who had a problem. As hard as he tried, his Spanish teacher seemed to have it in for him. From the way Ms. Sandoval seemed to cringe when she called his name for attendance to the accusations of not studying when he squeaked out his answer when called on, he felt picked on. Mike claimed he had been studying hard. He says he even had a tutor. Mike told me, "No matter what I did, when I felt her hateful stare, I would forget everything about Spanish!" Finally, one day in the middle of class while feeling unfairly criticized, he stood up, shouted how "lame" he thought the class (and his instructor) were, and stormed off to his counselor to drop the class. He received a failing grade and had to attend summer school to make it up. Ms. Sandoval, on the other hand, didn't lose any sleep over it.

Mike might have been right. Ms. Sandoval may have truly had it in for him. It does happen. Unfortunately, being right is seldom enough all by itself. He couldn't take responsibility for his teacher's attitude but he could have assumed the responsibility for fixing the situation. Mike could possibly have approached his teacher (after class) and addressed the situation in a proper manner, he could have shown her his efforts to study and be tutored, or perhaps he could arranged a meeting with Ms. Sandoval, his counselor, and himself before it escalated into an outburst in class. When he didn't, he ended up being the one that was hurt.

INVENT YOUR FUTURE

There is usually no point in being right and losing because of it. If you accept responsibility, not for someone being a jerk but for correcting the problem, you can usually come out ahead. Options become available to you. When you refuse responsibility you lose those options. Sometimes you have the option of being right or being happy.

Do you blame other people, the world, your background, school, the economy, or even your teacher that life doesn't always go the way you'd like? Do you complain that your parents screwed up, you just aren't smart enough, or you grew up on the wrong side of the tracks? With minimal effort, opportunity is out there waiting for you. You can change any part of your life or accomplish any goal as long as you are willing to accept that you are the one who is going to have to make the change!

ACTION STEP

Decide Today to Stop Passing the Blame

On the following page, make a list of circumstances for which you will no longer blame others and for which you are ready to accept responsibility. Following are some examples:

- My teacher does not appreciate my hard work.

- My lack of money is holding me back.

- My parents don't get along.

- People don't like me.

- My coach never puts me in.

- I just have a lot of bad luck.

- I can't control my temper.

- I want a car but don't have the money.

- I can't help the way I react.

- My parents drive me crazy!

INVENT YOUR FUTURE

Do you see the pattern? Now add at least ten items of your own to the list below. Take a few minutes.

1. _____

2. _____

3. _____

4. _____

5. _____

6. _____

7. _____

8. _____

9. _____

10. _____

If you're having trouble, ask yourself: What would a close friend add to the list? What would your teacher add? What would your mother add? Whether you agree with each item or not, once you have done all this, you will have a list personalized for you.

FIND THE SOLUTION

Looking back on your list, without necessarily accepting that you are responsible for an item, ask yourself if you were to accept responsibility, what type of action could you perform for each item on the list?

Could you do even better work?

Find out what your teacher really wants?

Find an after school job?

Could you get a tutor?

Sit down and talk – not yell – with your parents?

Ask an advisor for help?

Quit the sport that takes too much time?

The real answers are inside of you. The key is to accept responsibility for correcting the problem. Don't always try to be right or insist that life be fair. It is not. Stop whining and get on with it.

It's all about attitude. Your attitude is something – and sometimes the only thing – that you can control.

INVENT YOUR FUTURE

4. WHO NEEDS GOALS?

Let's pretend that one day, while relaxing around the house, you decided you need some ice cream. Not just any ice cream, but Ben & Jerry's Chunky Monkey ice cream. Nothing else would do. So you go the freezer and realize there is none. All you find is a leftover bag of stale pretzels. Bummer. (Hey! Who put pretzels in the freezer?) What would you do? You could decide that the stale pretzels will do. Or you could decide that there was no substitute for your Chunky Monkey craving. If you chose the pretzels, the job is easy. However, if you decided that nothing else would do but your favorite ice cream, then the adventure has just begun.

Before you go, you might need to get dressed, find your wallet or purse, brush your hair, and find a way to get to the store. If you drive, you may have to brave traffic, red lights, a speeding ticket, or an empty tank of gas. Maybe you don't have a license and have to ask your mom for a ride. Then, when you arrive at the store, you might find out it is closed or out of the ice cream you seek. This is what effective goal setting is all about. It starts with a desire and ends with the fulfillment of that desire.

Yet, in between there is plenty of action that may or may not keep us from the goal. (Just the thought of these obstacles make the pretzels sound better by the minute.)

THE LAW OF MOTIVATION

As we begin the adventure, the first step is to become familiar with what I call Russ Peak's 'Law of Motivation'. This law is adapted from the thoughts of well-known 17th century scientist, Sir Issac Newton. He's the guy who declared gravity when an apple fell on his head. Well, he also developed the groundbreaking First Law of Motion. It states that:

"An object at rest will remain at rest until acted upon by an outside force."

This means that unless you live on a hill, a bowling ball sitting on your front lawn is not going to go rolling away by itself. With some redefinition of terms, these words can have significant impact on our lives. We transform the Law of Motion into the Law of Motivation.

For our scenario, we will apply this scientific law to motivation and your life; the object will be defined as your goals, your desires, your dreams - the thing that you want to have come true. It could be anything big or small: the type of person you want to be, the grades you want to achieve, the friends you want to make, the job you want to land, the college you want to attend, the athletic ability you wish to attain, the money you want to earn. Anything! It is as simple as that!

The root of the word motivation is *motive*.

Here's how the dictionary defines motive:

Motive: something causing or able to cause motion.

Before you get yourself motivated you must have a motive - something to get you going. What is your goal? You must know what your goal is or you can't begin your path to success. If you have no object, you have nothing to put into motion. If you don't know what your goal is yet... don't worry we'll get you there!

So far the Law of Motivation says:

"Your goals and dreams will remain at rest unless acted upon by an outside force."

The second part of this law talks about an outside force. That's where you come in again. You are that force. Just as nobody can decide your goals for you, neither can somebody fulfill them for you, nor can your goals fulfill themselves. Although you may be surrounded by people who love you and want you to succeed in your life, they don't care about your goals as much as you do. They can't. They aren't you. They are busy enough as it is trying to get their own goals into motion to worry about your life. Nobody can get your object into motion besides you. You have to do it.

Let's look at Newton's law again, but this time substituting our own words. It states: "Your goals and dream are not going anywhere until you take responsibility and do something about it."

Sounds simple, doesn't it? Well, it is. It's no secret. This is nothing new. Basic skills of goal-setting have been around for years. You use them on a small scale every day with the simple tasks you face – like going to the store to get ice cream. However, studies show that still less than three percent of people use goal-setting skills where it really counts.

So many people step into the world and say, "I hope I end up somewhere good." Then ten years later the look back and declare, "Hey! I never ended up anywhere good!" That should come as no surprise. How can you end somewhere good if you have no idea where good is? That's what goal setting is all about - not letting life and chance decide where you end up, but instead making the choice by having goals having dreams, and inventing your future.

Remember those three percent that do use goal setting skills? Among them you'll find the top achievers of this world. It didn't take a magical cross. It only took the effort to spend the little time it takes to properly set goals. This is not the theory of motivation. It's the Law of Motivation. Like other scientific laws, this process does not only work in a few random instances. It can be repeated and duplicated by anyone who desires their goals and dreams to come true.

"The young do not know enough to be prudent, and therefore they attempt the impossible - and achieve it, generation after generation."

- Pearl S. Buck

5. WHAT DO YOU REALLY WANT?

Three weeks ago I arrived at the Bob Hope Airport in Burbank, California. While I was waiting for my suitcase at the baggage claim carousel I began to 'people watch' as I often do to pass the time. After a few minutes, I spotted someone worthy of my attention. He was a man in his early twenties sporting a foot tall jet black Mohawk. Sound rebellious? Well, he didn't stop there. He had transformed himself into a wonderful surreal work of art. From his wrist to his shoulder, his arms were sleeves of tattoos of every color and abstract shape imaginable. His forehead was inked as well with a gothic script I could not read. Piercings decorated this man until he resembled a Christmas tree. I counted fourteen rings on his left ear, twelve through his right, and each had one of those large disks that spread the lobe until the hole is about two inches in diameter. Eight large rings encircled his lower lip and on his eyebrows he had a pointed stud on the outer edges which made him look as though he had horns. As I took this all in one phrase entered my head: "NOW THAT'S COMMITMENT!!"

I really hope that guy enjoys his look because it's going to be there with him his entire life. There is no turning back. I can honestly say that I have never been so thoroughly committed to an ideal that I would transform my body into such a permanent symbol of that commitment. When I was in my twenties I changed who I was like I was changing socks. On Monday I might have spiked my hair and dressed all in black, Tuesday my favorite sports jersey, and by Friday I could have been wearing a polo shirt with khakis. But I donned nothing that I couldn't alter within a quick trip to the closet.

"As you become more clear about who you really are, you'll be better able to decide what is best for you - the first time around."

- Oprah Winfrey -

It took me a while to figure out who I was. But once I did, things got a little easier. It allowed me to reach for goals that suited me... not someone else. Could you imagine if one day that guy from the airport wakes up one morning and decides: "Hey! I think I want to be a preschool teacher!"? He might have his work cut out for him when he shows up to the interview. It's great to be committed but only if it's the right thing for you. That's why it's important to take your time and discover your likes and dislikes. So that you're headed off in the right direction. Furthermore, if you're like most people, the things you're into now will not be what you're into next year or maybe even next week. We all evolve and change as we experience new things. That's why about 80% of college students change their major at least once. On average, these students change their major three times over the course of their college career. Plus, most experts now predict that the average person will change careers three to five times over the course of his or her work life. So before you pierce and ink up, let's explore who you are with a few action steps that will lead you to discover what you really like.

INVENT YOUR FUTURE

Be who you are and say what you feel because those who mind don't matter and those who matter don't mind.

- Dr. Seuss

ACTION STEP

WHAT INSPIRES YOU?

What do you enjoy doing? Why? _____
_____
_____

What don't you enjoy doing? Why? _____
_____
_____

What kinds of subjects do you enjoy learning about? _____
_____
_____

If you could spend an hour with any person who ever lived, who would that be? What would you do? What would you ask?
_____
_____
_____
_____

INVENT YOUR FUTURE

What kinds of things do you care about? _____

_____

_____

_____

What do you like to read about?_____

_____

_____

What things are you better at than most people? _____

_____

_____

_____

What things have others told you you're good at? _____

_____

_____

_____

What do you often daydream about? _____

_____

_____

ACTION STEP

TAP INTO YOUR TALENTS!

Speaking   Writing   Listening   Humor   Music

Mechanical   Motivating   Decision making   Singing

Dancing   Working with people   Athletics   Creativity

Public speaking   Building things   Numbers   Leading

Using the talents listed above as well as your own, list ten talents that you possess. If you have trouble with this one... ask a friend or family member.

1. _____
2. _____
3. _____
4. _____
5. _____
6. _____
7. _____
8. _____
9. _____
10. _____

INVENT YOUR FUTURE

ACTION STEP

Let's say five years from now, the local news channel is going to do a story about you. Among other things, they are going to mention three specific details about you. What three things would you want them to say?

ACTION STEP

Off the top of your head, make a list of the top five things you really want. Not what your parents, friend, or teachers seem to want for you. Make a list of what is important to you. Write them in sentences like:

"I want to live by the beach."

or

"I want to learn how to play the guitar"

1. _____
   _____

2. _____
   _____

3. _____
   _____

4. _____
   _____

5. _____
   _____

INVENT YOUR FUTURE

Shoot for the moon. Even if you miss, you'll land among the stars.

- Les Brown

6. LET'S SET SOME GOALS

In that last chapter you explored your strengths and weaknesses. Your likes and dislikes. And before that you wrote your own statement defining what success means to you. Now let's learn the characteristics that make for a good goal. There are four important qualities of a goal:

1. **YOUR GOAL MUST BE POSITIVE**
2. **YOUR GOAL MUST BE SPECIFIC**
3. **YOUR GOAL MUST BE REACHABLE**
4. **YOUR GOAL MUST BE PERSONAL**

When I hear from teens that explain that they are having trouble with accomplishing their goals, it is usually because they started off wrong from the beginning. They had bad goals. I don't mean the things that they wanted were bad. It's just that they set up their goals improperly. If your goal doesn't satisfy these four requirements, you might run into some trouble along the way.

QUALITY #1: MAKE YOUR GOALS POSITIVE

Ever see one of those scenes in the movies where the hero is climbing or hanging from a high place? The hero's friend watching the situation unfailingly will shout "Don't look down!!!" What happens? The hero looks down and gets freaked out. To keep that from happening, what the friend should have shouted was "Keep your eyes forward!"

We tend to go the direction in which we are focused.

That's why driving class teaches that when a car with bright headlights approaches you should focus on the white line on the right side of the road. Not only does it provide you with a reference to keep your car on the road and reduce the recovery time your eyes will need when the other car passes - It keeps you from driving into the oncoming car. If you stare into the headlights you will subconsciously veer toward it.

In that same manner, successful goals are made stating the positive - not the negative. If you state your goals declaring the negative aspects, it will usually become the object of your focus.

LET'S SET SOME GOALS

Here are two examples:

    Positive goal: "I will receive a B or higher on my math test."

    Negative goal: "I hope I don't fail!"

OR

    Positive goal: "I will get along with my boss."

    Negative goal: "I won't let my boss get me mad."

When you state your goals highlighting the positive, you will quickly find yourself headed in the right direction.

"Life is 10% of what happens to me and 90% of how I react to it."

- John Maxwell

Quality #2: Make Your Goals Specific

Recently, at a middle school where I presented a goal setting workshop I asked the audience if there was anyone out there who had a goal for their life. Fourteen year old Lucas raised his hand and said, "Yeah! My goal is to be rich!" When I asked him how he was going to get rich he replied, "I don't know. I just want to be rich!" Unless Lucas gets a bit more specific, he doesn't have a goal. That's because there are so many ways that one can become rich. He could own his own business, become a surgeon, or perhaps he get there by winning the Lottery. In all these cases, being rich is more of an outcome from a goal than an actual goal.

If your goal is "to do better in school" you'll need to be a bit more specific since that can have so many meanings. There can be several reasons why you are not doing well. Do you have a certain class that needs attention? Are you having trouble focusing? Is it a social or discipline problem that should be the object of your goal?

Here are a few goals that might specifically state the situation:

>"My goal is to study at least one hour every day!"

>"My goal is to receive an A in History."

>"My goal is get along with my lab partner."

QUALITY #3: MAKE YOUR GOALS REACHABLE

Sometimes the quickest way to get burned out when pursuing a goal is when we feel like our goal is never going to happen. This is often because we have selected a goal which is way out of our reach.

I met a young lady named Samantha. She says her goal is to be the first female President of the United States. That is quite a notable goal! However, at this moment, Samantha is fifteen. Her goal might be a long ways off. It's not that Samantha couldn't be President; I have seen her determination and believe she could do it. However, the minimum age to be President is thirty-five years old. That's twenty years in the future. A lot could happen between now and then. Especially with five elections in the next twenty years, we might see a woman take her seat in the White House before Samantha has a chance. A better bet for Samantha's focus of energy might be something within her immediate control like becoming President of her eighth grade class, joining the debate team, being a volunteer for a local election, or preparing to get into the school that will take her in the direction of her grand political aspirations. All of these other goals are very important steps yet are within a reasonable distance for their success and less likely to lead to frustration.

QUALITY #4: MAKE YOUR GOALS PERSONAL

Making your goals 'personal' means that you need to strive for something that you can believe in. You've got to own your goal. This is a crucial detail vital to the success of your goals. If you are just going after what your parents, teachers, and family seem to want for you, you might be doomed to failure. You've got to be able to look at your goal and say, "That's mine!" Self-help author Stephen Covey puts it this way:

"Motivation is a fire from within. If someone else tries to light that fire under you, chances are it will burn very briefly."

Ashley was one of my closest friends from high school. She was a talented artist and an amazing photographer. Ashley's dream was to be a graphic designer. Her parents, however, had a different plan. With a viewpoint that such a career was a bit unstable, they pushed her away from art and when she went to college, she majored in accounting. As her friend, I knew this was one of the last things which would interest her. She explained that she was doing this to make her parents happy.

Three years into her career, Ashley finally admitted to herself as well as to her parents that she was miserable. She went back to school as an art major. Ashley is now an artist or 'Imagineer' working at Disney Studios. You may not know Ashley, but you have probably seen some of her work in your favorite Disney movies.

LET'S SET SOME GOALS

Take a few minutes and review what you have written in the action steps in chapters 2 and 5. Then, with the help of what you've written, along with the following action steps, get ready to write three goals that fit the four qualities outlined in this chapter.

These three goals will be **long-term goals**. That means that they are goals that you will be able to work on over a period of time, or that might take a few steps to get to. Well, talk about breaking down your goals in to those steps of **short-term goals** in the next chapter.

INVENT YOUR FUTURE

Teen friends tell us some of their goals:

> "My goal is to make first chair playing flute in the band."
>
> Angela, Age 16

> "My goal is to be accepted into Stanford University Business School."
>
> Thomas, Age 18

> "My goal is to earn enough money for my church youth group mission trip. We're going spring break!"
>
> Peter, Age 15

> "My goal is to get my homework grades up to a C (or better) so I can pass intermediate algebra."
>
> Bailey, Age 16

> "I want to get the supervisor position at the restaurant I work at."
>
> Lexi, Age 17

ACTION STEP

YOUR LONG-TERM GOALS

Using the action steps from the previous chapters as well as the tools we have learned to write successful goals, write your three long term goals in the spaces below.

Long-Term Goal 1

_____

_____

_____

Long-Term Goal 2

_____

_____

_____

Long-Term Goal 3

_____

_____

_____

INVENT YOUR FUTURE

ACTION STEP

In the spaces below, determine why the three long-term goals you've chosen are important to you.

Long-term goal 1 is important to me because...

Long-term goal 2 is important to me because...

LET'S SET SOME GOALS

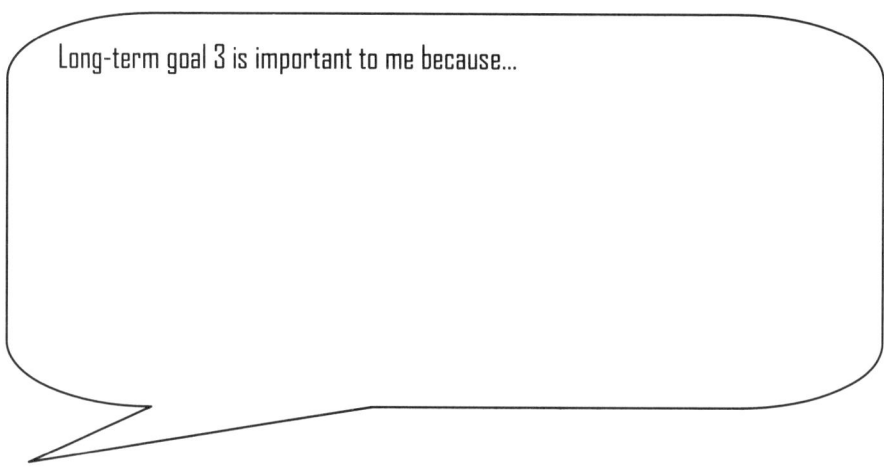

Congratulations! If you have found three specific goals that you have identified and know why they are important to you, you have accomplished more than eighty percent of your peers! Have you heard the saying, "Eighty percent of success is showing up."? We'll it's the same thing with goals. Figuring out what you want is usually the hardest part. When you've accomplished the last two action steps, you've "shown up." Now, remember these goals you've written. We will be coming back to them several times over the next few chapters.

INVENT YOUR FUTURE

7. BREAKING IT DOWN

When I turned sixteen, like every American boy I decided I needed a car. I had a job, my grades were okay, and I had nearly eight hundred dollars in the bank. That was more money than I had ever had to call my own and I felt as though I were a millionaire. Once I looked in the newspaper classifieds at cars, however, I quickly realized that even in the year 1986, eight hundred dollars was not a lot when it came to buying a car. The next morning, I found myself in a stranger's driveway looking at a 1980 Dodge Colt. This car was a dirt brown tin box on wheels. It was beautiful and priced at 850 dollars. I rushed home to tell my parents I found the car I was going to buy.

My dreams were shattered when my father looked up from his newspaper and simply asked me what the 'Blue Book' was on this car. Was it a good price? I had no idea. In fact, I didn't even know what a Blue Book was. After explaining that the Blue Book was a guide that tells how much a car is worth, he directed me to the library (That's where we went before the internet.) where I rushed to find the resident Blue Book and found all of the information. The current owner's price was pretty close to the low end and I was thrilled that I would be able to go home and tell Dad I had found a deal!

Without a hint of excitement at my discovery of the deal of the century, he asked, "What do the consumer magazines say about this car?" I was shattered. Luckily, this time I did not have to head to the library as Dad directed me to a stack of magazines. He told me I would find a current consumer car guide somewhere in the pile. Once again, I had victory as I reported to Dad that *Consumer Reports* magazine rated this car as reliable.

Then Dad asked, "What did the mechanic say about this car?" I couldn't believe the agony Dad was putting me through just because, as I was sure, he did not want me to have a car or a social life. It was a relief when everything checked out okay and I finally got the car.

About five years later, when I was ready to buy a real car (that is, a newer used car), I visited the family credit union to apply for a loan. The loan officer asked me, "Do you know what the Blue Book is on this car?" I looked across the desk at this woman who suddenly wore my father's face and said, "Yes," as I produced a file smartly labeled "car loan information." The file contained photocopies of the Blue Book, a copy of ads for five similar cars, the Consumer's Guide rating, as well as that of another car rating guide, a full report from the mechanic who checked out the car a few days earlier, and pay stubs from my current job. I was prepared and she even informed me that she was impressed at how thorough and organized I was. She explained to me that I had not yet achieved the type of credit needed to grant such a loan, but in the light that I seemed so responsible and knew what I was doing, she would make an exception.

When you have a clear destination and you know exactly what you need to get there, the road to what you want often gets smoother. Sometimes opportunities open for you quicker than when you stumble along like I did dealing with my dad on my first car buying experience. Because I had shown my loan officer that I was responsible enough to know how to find a proper car, she assumed that I would be responsible enough to pay back the loan. I didn't let her down.

"Baby steps count, as long as you are going forward. You add them all up, and one day you look back and you'll be surprised at where you might get to."

- Christopher Gardner

YOU KNOW WHERE YOU WANT TO GO. DO YOU KNOW HOW TO GET THERE?

As a traveler who is seldom in the same place from one day to the next, I have found that a large part of my job is to figure out where I need to be next. Sometimes my next appointment may be just across town; other times I need to jump on an airplane to my destination. I wasn't born with the map to the world in my possession but luckily, I live in a time where I can rely on my portable GPS unit to give me not only a map, but easy driving directions, mile tracking points, and even a time schedule. Without these tools, I would be lost.

Just as my GPS can help me get to my destination, you can find the path to your next destination with a little research. If there is a topic or a goal that interests you, find out everything you can about it. Read all of the information that you can get your hands on. Check out the infinite information resources on the internet. And most of all, talk to experts — people who have already made it to where you want to go. I was irritated with my dad for what he put me through, but the fact is that if he hadn't shown me the necessary steps to buying a vehicle, I wouldn't have been prepared when it came time for my loan. So, be open-minded. Don't be too proud or ignorant, thinking that you have all the answers. The sooner you do this, the sooner the path ahead of you will start to clear. You'll know where you need to go. There shouldn't be too many surprises up ahead.

Arriving at your goal is a lot like driving to a destination. There are stops and turns along the way. Sometimes getting from point A to point B requires that you first stop at point Q, W, L, back to A, then over to M. To make things less confusing, it best to narrow down your goals into smaller steps.

"To me, if life boils down to one thing, it's movement. To live is to keep moving."

- Jerry Seinfeld

High school junior Allie decided she would like to improve her grades in math. It's important to her because she knows she needs to get to the next math level for her senior year to get into her chosen college. That will require at least a B grade this semester. She is generally a good student but math isn't her strongest subject. Allie is sure she can tackle this challenge. She's clear on her goal. She knows why she wants it. Now she has to break it down to "how?"

INVENT YOUR FUTURE

Allie asked herself an important question: "How do I intend to improve my grade in math?" She then pulled out a piece of paper and wrote out her ideas.

---

1. By explaining to my teacher my desire to do better and maybe ask for help or advice.
2. By setting aside extra time for study and homework.
3. By going to the tutoring center and getting help.
4. By cutting back on television and internet time until I get past this hurdle.
5. By going to bed early the night before all tests and quizzes.
6. By asking for a seat at the front of the class to reduce distractions.

What Allie did was to break down her goal into steps. Most long-term goals, like the ones you set in the previous chapter need to be broken down into smaller steps. These are called **short-term goals.**

Just as with my goal to get dad's approval for a car, in order for Allie to accomplish her goal to receive a high math grade, there were several simple but important tasks she needed to accomplish in order for her to get there.

Who knows? With breaking her goal down and a little hard work, she might soon be able to add math to her list of strong subjects.

DEVELOPING SHORT-TERM GOALS

In order to establish the short-term goals that will lead to your major goal, you've got to keep asking the question "how?" This can be accomplished with three easy steps:

- Choose one of your long-term goals and ask yourself how you are going to get there.
- Make a list of how you are going to achieve your goal.
- Look at every step and ask yourself how you are going to go about carrying out that step.

For Example:

<u>My long-term goal:</u>

"Be a starter on my school's varsity soccer team"

<u>Steps I need to get there:</u>

- Practice every day
- Work out to improve my strength
- Run every day to improve my speed
- Eat a healthier diet

BREAKING IT DOWN

Now, I need to look at those short-term goals and figure break them down even further. Again we have to ask ourselves "how?" Just since I wrote down "Run every day" doesn't mean it'll be easy. I might have to ask myself:

"How will I fit running every day into my already busy schedule?"

I might have to plan it further like:

"Every morning I'll set my alarm an hour earlier than normal. I'll get up and run 30 minutes before breakfast."

There! Now that's a plan.

I might even need help with some of my short-term goals. I may not have a clue as how to: "Eat a healthier diet."

So I might have to ask the question: "How can I figure out what sort of a diet I should have?" Ask my coach? Read a book? See my doctor?

Now you try it!

ACTION STEP

Just like in the previous examples, ask yourself "How?" to create the short-term goals that will lead to your success.

On the line below, re-write one of your three long-term goals from the last chapter and ask yourself how you are going to get there.

Long-Term Goal:

_____

Now, make a list of how you are going to achieve your goal. We'll keep it simple and just do five for this exercise.

1. _____ *How?*

2. _____ *How?*

3. _____ *How?*

4. _____ *How?*

5. _____ *How?*

Finally, look at each of your five short-term goals and ask yourself how you are going to go about carrying out that step.

Okay, here's the next part.

Look at your long-term goal, and write a deadline for you to complete this goal. Then, look at the short-term goals you've written and declare a deadline for each step. You might find that your statements don't go in exact chronological order. Some steps might be ready for you to act on today, while others require the completion of one other step first. The important thing is that you get a time frame in mind.

On the following three **Goal Setting Forms**, go through the entire process. Re-write your long-term goals, your "Why?", and finally answer the question "How?" – Just like you did on that last exercise. Do this with all your goals. When you write down a goal you give it life!

Write it down. Writing goals have a way of transforming wishes into wants; cant's into cans; dreams into plans; and plans into reality. Don't just think it – ink it!

- Unknown

GOAL SETTING FORM

Long-Term Goal: _____

_____

_____
Deadline: _____

Why is this important to me? _____

_____

_____

#	STEP	Deadline
1		
2		
3		
4		
5		
6		
7		
8		
9		
10		

GOAL SETTING FORM

Long-Term Goal: _____

_____

_____

                              Deadline: _____

Why is this important to me? _____

_____

_____

#	STEP	Deadline
1		
2		
3		
4		
5		
6		
7		
8		
9		
10		

INVENT YOUR FUTURE

GOAL SETTING FORM

Long-Term Goal: _____
_____
_____
_____ Deadline: _____

Why is this important to me? _____
_____
_____

#	STEP	Deadline
1		
2		
3		
4		
5		
6		
7		
8		
9		
10		

BREAKING IT DOWN

Now that you've learned how to create and write out effective goals, remember that you can do this with all your goals - now and in the future. Go to my web site www.RussPeak.com and on the resources page, you can download every action step from this book, as well as more of these Goal Forms. Use them to help you outline your goals and to remind you of the necessary steps to invent your future. While you're at my site, make sure you sign up for my newsletter. I'd love to keep you up to date on the latest goal setting techniques!

The world is moving so fast these days that the man who says it can't be done is generally interrupted by someone doing it.

- Elbert Hubbard

8. JUST DO IT!

Once upon a beautiful Saturday morning, I decided it was time to clean out the garage. The clutter had piled up over the spring and it was difficult to make it from one side to the other. So I got up and got dressed to create a garage that I could be proud of. Stepping carefully into the garage, and surveying the surroundings, my enthusiasm quickly disappeared. The garage was truly a disaster. I turned back around into the house and turned on the XBOX instead. I was already defeated. I didn't even know where to begin.

Has this ever happened to you? If so, don't feel too bad. Many people, at the onset of their goal, look at the final outcome they desire and become overwhelmed with the tasks that lay before them. There are so many factors that seem crucial to their success that they have no idea where to begin. So they don't begin and are defeated before they have even started to act.

Keep It Simple

When a problem looks too big and complex, or when you're overwhelmed and there just doesn't seem to be a good place to start, you can begin by identifying simple components of the problem that can be solved. We did that when we created our short-term goals as smaller steps to our long-term goals. Solve them and remove them. Now there is less clutter and the total problem set has been simplified. You will discover that more simple problems may have been exposed and you've have to add them to the list. That's okay. Solve these and remove them. Repeat the process. You may be surprised to discover at some point only simple problems remain.

"An object at rest will remain at rest until acted upon by an outside force." — The Law of Motion

So far in this book we have primarily covered the first part of this law, looking for an object to move. Now we are going to move it. I told you earlier in this book that I wanted you to think big. I have told you there are no limits to your goals. I meant it. You might have even set a goal for yourself thinking, "I don't even know the first thing about this!" That's okay. You have time to figure all of that out as you go. The important thing is to ask yourself the following question:

"What can I do today that will bring me even a little closer to my goal?"

JUST DO IT!

Surely you believe there is something you can do that will change your life in a positive way and take you forward in your success. It doesn't even have to be a big something. If you have always wanted to be a doctor but have no idea what it takes, the first step might be to get online and check out what colleges are available, what the requirements are, and how much the tuition is. You might even call and have a catalogue sent to you. That won't make you a doctor yet, but at least you will have done the first step.

Or perhaps your goal is like Allie's and you need to get a tutor to improve your grades. Or, like our soccer example and I have yet to begin my daily run. Maybe you can take the first step today — it could be as simple as a phone call. Once you build a little momentum, the next step will be even easier. Pretty soon, before you know it, your goal will be complete.

What about my garage? Of course, I made it back out to that mess and picked out on area in which to start. I picked up a box and started sorting. By the end of the day, I could see the floor. By the end of the weekend, I could open the garage door without shame.

If you have a goal and you have made the choice for success, the most important thing for you to do right now is to decide what step you can do immediately to get your object moving — even if it's just an inch. Just do it! Immediately! Then do the same thing the next day and the next day. I guarantee soon your object will be in motion and you will be unstoppable.

Don't get caught up in all the details of a master plan before you take action. Don't worry if you don't yet know what step you will take tomorrow. Once you're off to a good start, you can start thinking and planning on a larger scale. The picture will become clearer and the map of where you need to go will appear.

Not Tomorrow... Now!

Perhaps you've heard this quote by Napoleon Hill: "Whatever the mind can conceive and believe, it can achieve." I believe in this concept and have referenced this quote in many of my motivational presentations. Yet the one factor that is missing is that just because you have conceived a goal and believe in your goal… that does not mean it is going to be achieved by itself. It is easy to get caught up in the planning of goals and the excitement of the possibilities. In fact, if you have set goals again and again and you can't figure out why you haven't reached them, the solution probably rests right here: The part that is missing in Mr. Hill's principle is that you need to take a risk and put out the effort and maybe even work your tail off for a while. Only then will your dream be achieved.

ACTION STEP

At this moment declare out loud the one thing that you can do today that would bring you closer to your goal. Then, before you go any further, put down this book and

JUST DO IT!

9. STAY ON COURSE

"People often say that motivation doesn't last. Well neither does bathing – that's why we recommend it daily."

- Zig Ziglar

Keeping your eyes on your path and making sure you don't get distracted from following its course can be difficult. This is especially true when you are constantly bombarded from all directions with alternate tasks that try to demand your attention as if the world depended on it. Some of these distractions deserve your attention while others are a waste of your time. Sometimes you will have to make sacrifices when opposing goals appear and you must make a choice. Just remember your goal. Remember your reason and your belief. Remember the steps you need to take in order see its success. You should have no problem making the right choice. It will be clear.

CHECK YOUR COURSE

As I mentioned before, I depend on my portable GPS navigation system to do my job. I use it to get to the school locations where I am to be speaking. This is great because I'm usually getting mentally prepared for my talk while I am driving and don't have time to try and figure out maps. Therefore, one of the features I appreciate the most is the fact that it tells me miles in advance that I will soon have to take action. For example it says: "Turn right on Wilson Street and go 15.6 miles." Then when I'm almost there it says: "In one mile turn left on Harbor Boulevard" This is great because whether I'm talking on the phone (with a hands free device of course), rocking out to the radio, or just in thought, I can prepare myself for the upcoming turn. In fact, my GPS refuses to let me stray from my goal. If I go off course, it instantly works on plotting a new course for me. It's relentless; it refuses to let me forget about my original destination, no matter how far off course I stray — even if I'm going in the opposite direction.

You might not have a portable GPS that keeps track of where you're going, but remember it's important to monitor your own progress and make sure you haven't missed a turn. Catch yourself on a daily basis and ask, "Is what I am doing right now going to lead me to the place I want to be?" Are you like most of America, watching six-and-a-half hours of television per day? Perhaps you are addicted to video games, social networking sites, or text messaging your friends. Are you wasting your time with meaningless tasks as you put off obtaining success?

MAKE SUCCESS A HABIT

When my oldest daughter Megan reached the second grade, every night during dinner, we would go through a daily ritual:

I would ask, "Megan, so what did you learn today at school?"

Megan's answer: "Nothing"

So I would reply: "Well then you'll have to go back tomorrow."

In an interview with best-selling author Leo Buscaglia, he explained that every night before he went to bed, his father would ask him, "What have you learned today?" If Leo couldn't give him an answer, his father would send him to the encyclopedias to learn something he could report to his father. He claims he still does this ritual every night.

Ask yourself, "What have I done today that will contribute to the accomplishment of my goal?" Decide what you can and will do next to guarantee that your dream will become reality

MAKE SURE YOU SEND A CLEAR MESSAGE

My other daughter Grace has a ritual of her own. She thinks she's really funny when I ask her a question and she answers a verbal "yes!" but shakes her head No at the same time. Okay, it is pretty funny but also really confusing because I don't know what her real answer is. Does she mean yes or no? After a few tries of this, I usually just exclaim that I will make the decision for her. Then I quickly get a straight answer.

"My theory is that if you look confident you can pull off anything - even if you have no clue what you're doing."

- Jessica Alba

Are you being held back from your goals because you are not being consistent in your life? When I went for my car loan, even if I had a briefcase full of paperwork yet had walked through my loan officer's door in tattered jeans, disorganized, and swearing like a sailor, would she have been able to take me seriously? The world is watching closely to catch you if you do not walk your talk.

BE LOYAL TO THE GOAL – THE PATH MAY CHANGE

At some point of your journey toward your goal, you may find that the path you are on was heading toward your goal but is now beginning to veer in another direction. That's quite okay. If you keep making checks as you travel your path, you'll notice it in time and be able to make the proper turn. Be flexible. Just like the driver who encounters a road-block or heavy traffic and then must find a detour, you may also need to find another path to get to your destination. Most people who have become, or "arrived at a point of success" didn't get there on one direct path. Usually it took many changes in course to get it right. Sometimes it will seem the path was going in a direction you would have never anticipated. If the road you've been on changes, take it in stride. Sometimes detours showing us even better routes to our destination.

Enjoy Your Goals

Most people wouldn't be able to tell you what they saw on their way home from work yesterday. Perhaps they would remember a particularly eye-catching billboard or a tragic accident, but if you asked them to describe the trees along the road or the shapes of the clouds in the sky, they would be at a loss. They were so busy trying to get home as quickly as possible they didn't stop to enjoy the beauty of the world that surrounds them.

> "Success is the journey, not the destination."

There's yet another person's definition of success. The unknown author gives us something to think about. No matter what your path may be, make sure you keep your eyes looking forward but enjoy the present too. Not only will it make your path more pleasant as you move along its course, but you'll find it seeming to go a lot quicker.

10. THE POWER OF BELIEF

One of my favorite stories that demonstrates the significance of belief is the record-breaking triumph of Roger Bannister. He was the first person to break the four-minute mile. This was an athletic conquest people had been trying to achieve since the ancient Greeks. (In fact, I found one article that stated the Greeks had lions chase runners to try and make them run faster. Of course, it didn't work for the Greeks. It did work great for the lions!) For thousands of years, everyone thought it was physiologically impossible for a human to run a mile in four minutes. Then on May 6, 1954, a British athlete named Roger Bannister proved everyone wrong. At a meet at Oxford University, he broke the four-minute mile completing it in 3 minutes 59.4 seconds, establishing a world record.

Perhaps more astounding is that this was bettered less than two months later by an Australian athlete named John Landy, who set a record of 3 minutes, 58 seconds. The next year, thirty-seven other runners broke the four-minute mile, and the year after that, three hundred runners broke the four-minute mile! Today the four-minute mile is accomplished on a regular basis by athletes without a second thought.

Why is it possible for so many to accomplish a feat thought to be impossible just a few decades ago? There have been no new training breakthroughs. Mankind did not increase its physical abilities. It was one simple ingredient: belief. Remember:

Psychological barriers or "Limiting Beliefs" are often profoundly more powerful than physical.

Roger Bannister believed in himself and in his goal. When it became a known fact that it was possible to break a four-minute mile, it was no problem for those who followed in his footsteps.

Nothing is impossible. Roger Bannister proved that when he refused to believe the experts and showed the world that if you set your goals, you can do anything. You may have a goal that everyone says is unrealistic. You may have people tell you to set your sights a little lower so you won't be disappointed. There might be others that laugh and say you possess a fool's dream. Next time they do, remember Roger Bannister, who refused to believe the doubters and changed the world.

You can change the world too. If you believe in yourself and in your goals, there is nothing you can't accomplish. Again, nothing is impossible.

BELIEVE IN YOURSELF

Beliefs are powerful allies. They may also be powerful foes. Your beliefs guide your actions and lay out the paths you will travel in your life. Your beliefs can give hope, or they can lead you to despair. I'm sure you've heard "Don't do drugs! They will tear down your mind." It's true! But it's also true that you can tear down your mind and sabotage your goals with a lack of belief in yourself. There have been many studies that prove this. Belief in oneself is a key element to the achievement of goals. One such study involved two groups of people taking the same class. One group is told that testing indicates that they all have exceptional aptitude for the subject and should do very well. The other group was led to believe that their ability was only average. The group who was labeled exceptional did much better than the group labeled "average," even though both groups were basically equal going into the study.

Look around. You must have at least one friend who achieves beyond her abilities because she thinks she can. You also probably have at least one friend who fails because he believes he will. Belief works both ways. It can help immensely or it can destroy your potential. What kind of beliefs will benefit you?

INVENT YOUR FUTURE

I'M THE GREATEST!!

I figured that if I said it enough,
I would convince the world that
I really was the greatest.

- Muhammad Ali

ALLOW OTHERS TO BELIEVE IN YOU

Beliefs also have a strong effect on how other people react to you. In another experiment by researchers Robert Rosenthal and Lenore Jacobson, a group of teachers were falsely told that certain students were tested and found to be "in a period of rapid intellectual growth." In other words, they were told that these kids were really, really smart. In reality, the students had been selected at random. At the end of the experiment, researchers reported that these students exhibited performance on IQ tests which was extraordinarily better than the scores of other students of similar ability and to what would have been expected these students without the extra attention. Why would this be? Maybe the teacher spent a little more time with the "above-average potential" student, tried a little harder, listened more closely to questions, paid attention. After all, they were special and deserved more attention. Maybe you should take advantage by subtly letting your teacher or others with power to affect your future that you have "above-average potential." It works. If you believe it, they probably will too.

Now that you have learned a few facts about beliefs, you may have a better understanding of why creating and cultivating positive beliefs about yourself and causing others to have positive beliefs about you is essential to success.

You Are In Charge Of Your Beliefs

Teen leader Justin had just arrived at the state student leadership convention in Nevada. The bus ride to the conference site was brutal. It took three and a half hours. Plus, he had been up all night in thought because he was running for state secretary of the conference's association. By the time he arrived, Justin was wiped out. His head ached and he decided that he would quickly check into his room and sleep the day away and start fresh tomorrow. He believed that he was too tired to learn anything or do his political desires any good. On his way to his room, however, Justin decided to change his attitude and his belief. Despite his doubts, he was determined to believe that he could and must go out and participate in the conference. He put a smile on his face, picked up his step and walked right into the main hall.

Justin knew that you can determine your beliefs as well as your attitude. They are closely linked. When there are negative beliefs that seem to be holding you back from what needs to be done, it is usually not very difficult to take steps to fix the situation.

First Justin asked himself what negative beliefs were holding him back. His answer: He believed that he was too tired to gain anything from the conference. He believed that he might lose the election for which he had worked so hard. He believed it would be impossible to have a good time with the way he felt.

Now, with his negative beliefs exposed, he asked himself which positive beliefs did he possess that would overcome the negative?

Here is what Justin came up with:

1. He believed that this opportunity to enjoy a conference was too good to pass up. (He had waited all year for it!)
2. He believed he could make it through the day even though he felt a little sleep deprived. He had stayed up many nights with friends in the past and made it through the day.
3. He believed that seeing friends at the conference he had not seen in quite a while would put him in a better mood.
4. He believed that he was, in fact, the most qualified and dedicated person for the position of state secretary.
5. He believed that there were possibly other students who had arrived equally tired, and that his positive attitude might influence them.
6. He believed that if he was going to be elected to his desired position, he needed to be seen at the conference.

INVENT YOUR FUTURE

Justin told me about this process he went through at the conference. He then said that within seconds of entering the hall he saw the smiling faces of several old friends, he talked with people about his election, and he saw that there were some great sessions he was glad he wasn't going to miss. Once he removed the psychological barriers, he soon discovered that his nervousness, his fatigue, and his headache all disappeared. Justin took charge by deciding what beliefs were going to influence his day and had a great conference. By the way, he won his election too.

ACTION STEP

List at least ten beliefs about yourself that are helpful—things like "I am intelligent," "I am a problem solver," "I relate well to people." Make sure you truly believe them.

1. _____

2. _____

3. _____

4. _____

5. _____

6. _____

7. _____

8. _____

9. _____

10. _____

ACTION STEP

List at least ten beliefs about yourself that are harmful — things like "I am not a self-starter," "I don't like talking to people," or "I'm just no good at math." Make sure you truly believe them.

1. _____
2. _____
3. _____
4. _____
5. _____
6. _____
7. _____
8. _____
9. _____
10. _____

ACTION STEP

Look back on these beliefs (both positive and negative). Can you see how these beliefs you listed make you who you are? Write a few sentences below describing in what ways can you see their influence?

_____
_____
_____
_____
_____
_____
_____
_____
_____
_____

INVENT YOUR FUTURE

ACTION STEP

List at least ten beliefs about yourself that you would like to have. They don't have to be true now. The idea is to make them true.

1. _____

2. _____

3. _____

4. _____

5. _____

6. _____

7. _____

8. _____

9. _____

10. _____

ACTION STEP

List at least ten beliefs about yourself that you want others to believe. Things like has above average potential, is a winner, has a great style, is responsible, and so on.

1. _____

2. _____

3. _____

4. _____

5. _____

6. _____

7. _____

8. _____

9. _____

10. _____

DO NOT BE HELD BACK BY FALSE BELIEFS

As hard to accept as it may seem, you might currently be holding on to a belief, or many beliefs, that are completely false. These inaccurate beliefs may be limiting your potential to achieve levels of significance and you don't even realize it. Such beliefs might include insecurity and a lack of confidence to try out for that position on the team that, when in reality, it could be yours if you just went for it. It may be a false belief in potential rejection that may cause you never to ask that special someone to the dance, audition for a play, or to run for a student office. Without check, these beliefs can keep you from reaching your full potential. Therefore, it is important that you sort through your beliefs and define where each of your beliefs may or may not lead you. You will find that your beliefs may be leading you down the wrong path.

ACTION STEP

Identify the false beliefs that limit your potential

Pick out either one of your three long-term goals or one of your short-term steps from your list that has been waiting for you to take action? Often it is simply a belief that has held you back.

Write it down:

_____

_____

Now, take a look at that goal you've chosen and ask yourself:

"What is the belief that is keeping me from achieving this goal?"

OR

"What is the belief that has held me back from pursuit of my goal?"

INVENT YOUR FUTURE

For example, you might answer something like:

I never signed up to be part of student senate because I don't feel as though I am popular enough to fit in.

I never took steps to join the campus newspaper because I can't believe that others would be interested in reading what I have to say.

Your answers might surprise you. Write them down:

_____

_____

_____

_____

_____

_____

_____

_____

Next ask yourself: "What belief must I embrace that will guide me to achieve my desired goal?" Write them down.

For example:

I may not be as popular, but I have just as much right, and even more to offer student senate than the people I see in charge now.

I have the skills and the desire to find the topics that will catch the eye of every student (and staff member too!) on this campus.

_____

_____

_____

_____

_____

_____

_____

_____

_____

Now that we've defended one of our goals from being attacked by negative beliefs, ask yourself what negative beliefs have kept you from your other goals? You can do this with all your goals.

When you have your true feelings written down and in a form that you can step back and look at, you might discover that you don't really believe what you just wrote. And if your belief does happen to be true, you have now identified it and now have something to work on. Just because it's true, doesn't mean that with a little hard work you can't change it. You might just have one more goal or step to add to the list.

11. CLEAN UP YOUR ACT

When I was fifteen, I bought and read a regulation army manual on survival behind enemy lines. The survival scenarios addressed in this particular manual were geared toward the situations of Vietnam-based military personnel who had managed to escape a prisoner of war camp. I couldn't imagine a more dangerous situation: behind enemy lines, with nothing but your bare hands for tools in your fight for survival. The manual covered topics of making traps and weapons, finding food and water, creating shelters, starting a fire, and so forth.

One section that really caught my attention was based on preparation for escape. The manual recommended stealing as much equipment as you could from your prison before you escaped — not that there would be much to steal. The first thing on the list was to secure a razor blade. Of course, that made perfect sense to me. You would need a blade to sharpen weapons, make a trap; cut your food... the possibilities were endless. However, as I read on, I was surprised when the section instructed the escapee to not use the blade for any of these obvious reasons. It instead gave instructions that the blade be used only for shaving. The soldier was instructed to give himself a shave, a haircut, and a bath as soon as it was possible.

At the time, yet to have shaved my first whisker, this made absolutely no sense to me. It does now. The manual was guiding the soldier into the proper mindset for extreme survival. In a prisoner-of-war situation, the prisoners were likely undernourished, injured, and psychologically defeated from the traumatic experiences of the camp. After the war, reports from actual POWs included detailed accounts of psychological attacks geared at destroying the morale of the prisoners. The prisoners were left unshaven, un-groomed, and filthy. This psychological mistreatment was purposeful on the part of the captors. They wanted the prisoners to be mentally as well as physically defeated. This could keep them from having the motivation to try an escape. And even if they were to escape, they would not survive because they were mentally and emotionally wiped out.

For some people, the day does not truly begin until they have stood under a shower and allowed the warm water to soak over their body. After a long day, some find that a direct trip to a hot bath to soak away their stress is exactly what they need before being able to relax for the evening.

CLEAN UP YOUR ACT

The manual directed the escapee to shave and take a bath because the only way to survive such a situation was to achieve a positive mindset. The writers of the survival guide wanted the soldier to feel refreshed and renewed. They wanted him to wake up and achieve a clear level of thinking, which would drive him to achieve and to survive.

Are there any areas of your life could use a good "cleaning up"? Maybe it's your current appearance or dress, the places you hang out, or the company you keep. As you plan for the success, you must thoroughly examine the productivity of these factors. When you embark on a new mission, just like the prisoner of war, you need to wash yourself clean of the grime that will hold you back and keep you from thinking clear. Furthermore, you need to stay clean, no matter what the cost. It is often the case with addicts and alcoholics who want to change their lives. They fail because they continue to attend the same parties and hang out with the same friends who are destined to bring them down.

My friend Anthony is a recovering alcoholic. He doesn't go to bars anymore because as he says:

"If you hang out in a barber shop long enough, you're bound to get a haircut!"

It's funny but it's true. Sometimes it's is necessary for you to break all ties, make new friends, get rid of your distractions, or change your life patterns completely to achieve the clear level of thinking you need to accomplish your goals.

ACTION STEP

The first step to breaking the bonds of negative behaviors or distractions in your life is to identify them.

Write down ten or more factors (bad habits, bad influences, bad behaviors) in your life are current threats to the success of your goals? Ask yourself what can you do to avoid, or eliminate, these threats?

1. _____

2. _____

3. _____

4. _____

5. _____

6. _____

7. _____

8. _____

9. _____

10. _____

ACTION STEP

Like the soldier's smooth shave... What are some healthy, positive habits you can add to your daily life to help you escape a motivational rut? How will each of these new habits improve your path to success?

1. _____

2. _____

3. _____

4. _____

5. _____

6. _____

7. _____

8. _____

9. _____

10. _____

INVENT YOUR FUTURE

12. IGNITE YOUR IMAGINATION

If you could have the fanciest car you desired and money was no object, what would it be? The fastest sports car? Something luxurious? An SUV? Perhaps you'd like to restore and cruise the town in a "classic"?

My neighbor Emilio's pride and joy is his brand new Mercedes. Even in this day of inflated prices, when he pulls up to the gas station to fill it up, he doesn't use the same cheap gasoline that I would put in my car. Instead, he uses premium grade. On Saturdays, you can always find Emilio in his driveway wiping down his baby with a cloth diaper. He makes sure it receives its proper tune-ups and oil changes on a regular basis. Nothing but the best!

Your mind is vast and seemingly infinite - an incredible wonder of the world. Nothing can even compare. It is constantly gathering information from everything around you. Every sound, smell, or touch, every conversation, every book you read, every movie you watch, every song you hear. And once it is recorded in your mind, it stays in... forever.

The constant input of data filling your mind transforms the way you think and the way you will be. It creates the person you are – your morals, your values, and your character. Doesn't that warrant a little extra tender loving care? Your mind is a "sweeter ride" than even the fanciest car, truck, or SUV.

Moreover, your mind is irreplaceable. You don't get another. Doesn't it make sense that when it comes time to give it fuel that you would choose the most premium grade? You should be filling your mind with information and ideas that will cause you to expand and explore the world around you, and maybe more important, the world within you. It's not hard. Even if it's just moments each day spent toward helping your mind grow you will notice the change in your awareness, your progress in life, and your attitude. The first place to begin is by reading books.

Edward P. Morgan writes:

"A book is the only place in which you can examine a fragile thought without breaking it, or explore an explosive idea without fear it will go off in your face. It is one of the few havens remaining where a man's mind can get both provocation and privacy."

So turn off the TV. Put your online chats on hold. Find a comfortable chair. And read. There are over two million books on the Books in Print directory. That's two million books full of ideas and thoughts, just waiting for you to explore. You can find books on any subject you might desire. Make sure you read a broad variety of books to get your mind working and your imagination soaring.

Did you know thirty-five percent of the American population has never entered a book store. Personally, I find this a shame. One study claims that eighty percent of all college graduates pick up less than one nonfiction book a year after graduation? Our minds do not stop craving enrichment once we receive our diplomas.

Most of these people use the excuse that they just have no time to read. If this is your situation, audio books are a wonderful substitute. In fact, when it comes to many types of books, you might find it preferable that they are in the form of audio books. Keep a library of motivational and inspirational CDs in your car or fill your iPod or MP3 player with their wisdom. As you drive to school, or hang out during lunch, take a detour from the regular tunes on your playlist and pick an audio of your favorite speaker, your favorite morning devotional, or something that will take your mind in a positive direction. It sure can make the day go a lot better.

FIND A MENTOR TO GIVE YOU GUIDANCE

Let's get back to your dream car. If you were to pick up the maintenance manual for your car and had no mechanical experience, it might first appear easy as you breeze through the diagrams and the troubleshooting steps. But when you open the hood of your vehicle, you will most likely see a sight that looks nothing like the illustrations in the book.

Books can't do it all. To excel in your learning, you need to have human interaction and guidance. Whether a formal teacher or an experienced peer, you need to have someone to model yourself after, to bounce ideas off of, and to explain things to you in a manner that will suit your own personal learning style.

You can find mentors by looking around you. An old proverb says, "When the student is ready, a teacher will appear." I guarantee you will find that you are surrounded with possibilities if you will just look hard enough. If all else fails join groups or clubs related to your goals and interests. You can look around your community, or perhaps there is already a club that fits your needs on your campus. If your school does not yet offer a group that matches your interests, maybe it's time for you to start one.

First comes thought; then organization of that thought, into ideas and plans; then transformation of those plans into reality. The beginning, as you will observe, is in your imagination.

- Napoleon Hill

CATCH ALL OF YOUR IMPORTANT THOUGHTS

Once you've stimulated your mind, you'll find it working more effectively. Creativity will begin to flow in just a short period of time. Keeping a journal is a great way to sort through your thoughts and explore the possibilities. Free write. Give yourself exercises or questions to answer. Re-do each of the exercises you have been given in this book and create your own questions to explore too. If this is done on a regular basis and you compared them over time, you will see evidence of how you have changed and grown.

With the miracles of technology, another great investment is a mini digital recorder. Many cell phones and MP3 players already have this feature. You can record good ideas whenever they pop into your head. And once you've got them down, it will make room in your mind for even deeper thinking.

ACTION STEP

List the last 4 books or magazines you've read (not assigned by your teacher), the 4 last movies you've watched, and the 4 most listened to tracks on your iPod or MP3 player. Then ask yourself: "Did this activity bring me closer to the person I strive to be?" Why or why not?

Last 4 Books

1._____

2._____

3._____

4._____

Last 4 Movies

1._____

2._____

3._____

4._____

INVENT YOUR FUTURE

4 Most Listened to Songs

1. _____

2. _____

3. _____

4. _____

ACTION STEP

Write the names of every possible person that you can use as a mentor—someone whom you respect and whose judgment you trust. Write down the reasons they would be a good mentor.

Name:_____

    Why?_____

Name:_____

    Why?_____

Name:_____

    Why?_____

Name:_____

    Why?_____

ACTION STEP

Think back to one of your three long-term goals and pick one that might be accomplished more effectively with a mentor. Give this some careful thought. Then in the spaces below, assign either the characteristics of an ideal mentor for that goal or a name if you already have someone in mind who meets your criteria.

Goal   Good Characteristics for Mentor

#1 _____

#2 _____

#3 _____

#4 _____

#5 _____

13. KEEP MOVING FORWARD

"Around here, however, we don't look backwards for very long. We keep moving forward, opening up new doors and doing new things - because we're curious. And curiosity keeps leading us down new paths. We're always exploring and experimenting."

- Walt Disney

I love my job as a speaker! In the last ten years, I have had the privilege to entertain and motivate over two million people across the nation. These audiences have included students, families, business people, celebrities, and incredible folks from every walk of life. One of my favorite parts of being a speaker, is that I have so many opportunities to meet new people and learn about new ideas from the most incredible sources. I have shared banquet tables with some of America's greatest successes and I love to hear their stories. One evening, I had dinner with a man named Charles P. Berolzheimer. Here is his story:

Mr. Berolzheimer, president of California Cedar Products Company, had a big problem. It began with his company, which generated, among other wood-manufacturing operations, more than four billion pencils per year. His problem was the high cost of disposing of waste that came from making these wood products, which was the cedar sawdust that was left after the pencils were completed. This sawdust cost the company quite a bit since they had to pay large sums to have it burned or hauled away to landfills.

The president of the company looked at this problem in a critical manner and discovered that if he were to mix this sawdust with petroleum wax and shape it into a log, it made an excellent effective alternative fireplace fuel to natural wood. It burned for at least four hours. Mr. Charles P. Berolzheimer is now president of Duraflame Firelogs, which is America's number-one selling fire log brand.

Have you ever heard the saying, "One man's trash is another man's treasure."? This guy literally took his company's trash - something that was a threat to the success of their financial future - and brilliantly turned it into their biggest success.

It was accomplished by thinking outside of the box. Something as simple as sawdust was transformed from obstacle into opportunity.

DETERMINATION

If you were to approach any one person in the world, present or past, whom you consider a success, what one thing would you ask them? This person could be a president, a businessman, a writer, an athlete, or anyone else you can think of who has taken his or her life to a level you would like to be. Perhaps you would ask them to what they attribute their success. I can guarantee they would tell you that one of the secrets, if not the number one secret to success is DETERMINATION! That means never give up, even when things look bad! You have the power to create your goals and plans - it just takes time.

Remember Newton? He had another Law of Motion too. It states that:

"An object in motion stays in motion unless acted upon by an outside force."

Remember that the object is your goal and you are the force. Nothing can stop your object's motion except for you. So don't let it. You have already learned that each individual is always responsible for his or her own reactions. Although tough times may come, you must make the decision to never give up on your goal.

KEEP MOVING FORWARD

One of the biggest downfalls of most would-be successes comes when it is time to put their ideas to the test. They give up the first time they see an obstacle. This often happens when their first voice of criticism emerges. Many just give up rather than face their fears that someone might not like their idea. Consider some of the following criticism:

> "This 'telephone' has too many shortcomings to be seriously considered as a means of communication. The device is inherently of no value to us."
>
> Western Union internal memo, 1876

> "We don't like their sound, and guitar music is on the way out."
>
> Response to the music of The Beatles in 1962

> "A cookie store is a bad idea. Besides, the market research says America likes crispy cookies, not soft and chewy cookies like you make."
>
> The response to Debbi Field's idea of starting Mrs. Field's Cookies

INVENT YOUR FUTURE

> "Who wants to hear actors talk?"
>
> Warner Brother's' H. M. Warner, 1927

> "You need to pass on being a part of *Speed*. It's a 'bus movie!'"
>
> To Sandra Bullock about the movie that grossed: over $350 million and set her career into motion.

> "I think there is a world market for maybe five computers."
>
> Thomas Watson, Founder of IBM

And I think this one is my favorite:

> "Everything that can be invented has been invented."
>
> Commissioner of Patents, 1899

Often, the best way to succeed is just jump in and don't give up.

Don't forget that many of the world's most incredible adventures were met with criticism. Who knows? The goal you have chosen to pursue may sound crazy or seem hopeless at times. But it could also be the best idea you have ever had.

TRUST IN YOUR GOALS!

BELIEVE IN YOUR GOALS!

NEVER GIVE UP!

It could change your life, or it could even change the world!

INVENT YOUR FUTURE

THE BUILDER

I saw them tearing a building down
A team of men in my hometown.
With a "Heave!" and a "Ho!" and a "Yes! Yes!" yell,
they swung a beam and a sidewall fell.

I asked the foreman, "Are these men skilled?"
"As the ones you'd use if you had to build?"
The man replied, "Oh no, indeed...
the most common labor is all I need...
because I can destroy in a day or two
what takes a builder ten years to do."

So I asked myself as I went on my way...
Which one of these roles am I willing to play?
Am I one who is tearing down
as I carelessly make my way around?
Or am I one who builds with care,
so that my world is a
little better... because I was there?

ANONYMOUS

14. A FEW LAST WORDS

Thank you for taking the time to read this book. I hope that you found it worthwhile. Although I have been a professional speaker for over a decade, this is first attempt as an author. It was quite a task. I've learned that speaking and writing are very different things. It was also a valuable reminder to me of the processes of goal setting and determination that I have attempted describe throughout these pages.

However, I felt as though I had to write it. This is because I honestly believe that you have the ability to accomplish anything that you set your mind to. I hope that you'll believe it too. Too many teens give up their aspirations for the extraordinary, not because they don't deserve it, but because they don't know how. This world is tough and filled with obstacles that can distract you from who you are and what you want to achieve. We need all the help we can get.

INVENT YOUR FUTURE

I am confident that if you took the time to read this entire book and to really do the action steps, you that you can overcome anything that might stand it your way.

Also remember that as the *The Builder* poem illustrates, you can use your life and your talents to build up the world... or you can tear it down.

It's easy to tear down. We see it all around us - on the news, in our neighborhoods and school, and even among friends and family.

As you set out to Invent Your Future, challenge yourself to be a builder. Build your life toward the positive. Build up your community, your family, and everyone with whom you come it contact. Build incredible things that change the world we live in. Use the tools that you've learned though this book to define who you are and go after the extraordinary! I know you can. And when you do, I'd love to hear about the great things that you are doing in your life. Email your stories and adventures to: myfuture@russpeak.com Who knows? Maybe I'll be able to use your story in my next book or edition of this one.

Good luck in all that you do!

Sincerely,

Russ Peak

RECOMMENDED READING

No matter what happens in your life. It doesn't matter if you're a 'book reader' or not. Whether you are college bound, starting a family, or going right into your chosen career. Keep growing your mind. Never stop learning. Never stop exploring new ideas. Knowledge is power. I promise you that continued reading will be a major key to inventing you future.

The following are a series of books that I would recommend to you to take your life to the next level. (In alphabetical order)

How to Speak and Listen Effectively, Harvey A Robbins, © Amacom, 1992. Although this book claims to be written with the business person in mind, it will give you a practical understanding of how people communicate and lets you develop and strengthen your own skills.

Over The Top, Zig Ziglar, © Thomas Nelson, 1997. This is just a great motivational book written the man who was one of my main inspirations to become a speaker. He's written several books but this is the one that I will pick up again and again. I also own the audio version and know that if I need a 'pick me up', this is it.

The 7 Habits of Highly Effective Teens: The Ultimate Teenage Success Guide, Sean Covey, © Simon & Schuster, 2000. Sean Covey takes his dad Steven's concepts that have shaped corporations world-wide and applies them to the teen life. If it worked for the big-wigs of America, it might work for you.

The Teenager's Guide To School Outside The Box, Rebecca Greene, © Free Spirit Publishing, 2001. If you're feeling boxed in by high school, this book is for you, this book is for you. It describes a world of alternate learning opportunities, then explains how to scout them out, how to decide what's right for you, how to prepare, what to expect, how to overcome barriers, and how to make the most out of whatever you do.

What Teens Need To Succeed: Proven Practical Ways to Shape Your Own Future, Peter L. Benson, © Free Spirit Publishing Inc., 1998. This giant book is written in the 'Dummies' type format. It is filled with over 1,200 ideas for building success at home, at school, in your community, in your congregation, and with your friends.

Winning People Over: 14 Days To Power And Confidence, Burton Kaplan, © Prentice Hall, 1996. Filled with self-tests and easy to do exercises, this is a great guide creating positive relationships with your peers and much more.

ABOUT THE AUTHOR

Russ Peak is an award-winning motivational speaker, entertainer, and leadership trainer who, for over a decade, has used his talents to entertain and inspire teens at student conferences and schools nationwide.

When he is not speaking Russ enjoys exercising, going to the beach, walking his beagle, and spending time with his family.

Find more about Russ Peak at:

www.RussPeak.com

Russ Peak's Most Popular Keynote

Use Your Mind ™

That's...

M for Motivation

I for Imagination

N for Navigation

D for Determination

GET READY FOR HIGH-ENERGY MOTIVATIONAL FUN!

Russ Peak walks on stage like any other motivational speaker. Yet he carries with him a few simple items -- a pen, a newspaper, a drawing pad, and a few envelopes. Then right from the start, he proceeds to capture the imaginations of the whole audience as they realize Russ is going to lead them through an interactive and mind-boggling experience that they will never forget! You see...

Russ Peak is recognized as one of the world's most skilled mentalists or "thought readers"!

When Russ Peak takes the stage, it's not just a performance -- it's a mind-blowing presentation of the "IMPOSSIBLE".

Unspoken thoughts are revealed from the minds of spectators, the outcome of impossible situations are correctly predicted, unseen designs are drawn and duplicated, and borrowed objects are used in ways that can be only explained as unbelievable!

Yet Russ clearly explains to the audience that he is not psychic, nor does he possess ESP, or any extraordinary or supernatural powers. Russ Peak is a MAGICIAN OF THE MIND. He uses these demonstrations of seemingly extraordinary powers to captivate, entertain, inspire, and teach that:

If you put your mind to it...

ANYTHING IS POSSIBLE!

Russ explains: "I don't have ESP or Psychic Powers. No supernatural force told me what to write. That prediction came true because I decided what I wanted to happen in this room today and MADE it happen. You can go through life trying to predict the future... hoping and guessing what might happen tomorrow. Or you can decide what you want, go after it, and INVENT THE FUTURE!"

The USE YOUR MIND keynote is a truly transformational presentation. Your audience will be both entertained and motivated as they learn real-life goal setting skills in a one-of-a-kind presentation that is filled with humor, magic of the mind, and an incredible high-energy message that is guaranteed to take their minds and actions from the ordinary to the extraordinary!

You can bring Russ Peak to your campus or convention!

Call Russ Peak Presentations
Toll Free: **800.381.5858**

Or, Check out his web site: www.RussPeak.com for reviews, online demo videos, and more!

BOOK ORDER FORM

Invent Your Future by Russ Peak

QUANTITY [ ] x 14.00 = [ ]

QUANTITY DISCOUNTS AVAILABLE. CALL FOR INFO.

Shipping Address

Name: [ ]

Street: [ ]

City: [ ]

State: [ ]

Zip Code: [ ]

Telephone: [ ]

Email: [ ]

INVENT PUBLISHING

P.O. Box 207 McMinnville, Oregon 97128

PHONE: 503.474.1464   FAX: 503.474.0287

www.InventPublishing.com

NOTES

NOTES